UNIVERSES Large AND Small

NUCLEAR ENERGY

Please visit our web site at: **www.garethstevens.com**
For a free color catalog describing Gareth Stevens Publishing's list of
high-quality books, call 1-800-542-2595 (USA) or 1-800-387-3178 (Canada).
Gareth Stevens Publishing's fax: (877) 542-2596.

Library of Congress Cataloging-in-Publication Data

Nuclear energy.—North American ed.
   p. cm. — (Discovery Channel school science: physical science)
   Originally published: Bethesda, Md.: Discovery Enterprises, 1999. React.
   Summary: Examines the discovery and creation of nuclear energy, its uses,
both beneficial and destructive, and the hazards of radioactive waste. Includes
related activities.
   ISBN-10: 0-8368-3362-7   ISBN-13: 978-0-8368-3362-1 (lib. bdg.)
   1. Nuclear energy—Juvenile literature. [1. Nuclear energy.] I. Title.
II. Series.
QC792.5.R43   2003
333.792'4—dc21   2002030533

This edition first published in 2003 by
Gareth Stevens Publishing
A Weekley Reader® Company
1 Reader's Digest Road
Pleasantville, NY 10570-7000 USA

This U.S. edition © 2003 by Gareth Stevens, Inc. First published in 1999
as *React: The Nuclear Energy Files* by Discovery Enterprises, LLC, Bethesda,
Maryland. © 1999 by Discovery Communications, Inc.

Further resources for students and educators available at
www.discoveryschool.com

Designed by Bill SMITH STUDIO
Project Editors: Justine Ciovacco, Lelia Mander, Sharon Yates, Anna Prokos
Designers: Nick Stone, Sonia Gauba, Bill Wilson, Darren D'Agostino,
  Joe Bartos, Dmitri Kushnirsky
Photo Editors: Jennifer Friel, Scott Haag
Art Buyers: Paula Radding, Marianne Tozzo
Gareth Stevens Editor: Betsy Rasmussen
Gareth Stevens Art Director: Tammy West

Printed in the United States of America

2 3 4 5 6 7 8 9 10 10 09

Writers: Jackie Ball, Michael Burgan, Nancy Cohen, Stephen Currie, Vanessa Elder.

Editor: Lelia Mander.

Photographs: Cover, Bill SMITH STUDIO; p. 2, painting of first chain reaction,
© Chicago Historical Society; p. 3, world motif, MapArt,
Pierre and Marie Curie, © Archive Photos; pp. 4-5, painting of
first chain reaction, © Chicago Historical Society; p. 8, Albert
Einstein, © UPI/CORBIS-Bettmann; Pierre and Marie Curie, J.
Robert Oppenheimer (both), © Archive Photos; p. 9, Enrico
Fermi, Dwight Eisenhower (both), © Archive Photos; pp. 10-11
Albert Einstein (both), © UPI/CORBIS-Bettmann; p. 12, *Enola
Gay*, © Archive Photos, John Hersey, © Brown Brothers, Ltd.;
p. 13, Hiroshima after the atomic bomb, © Archive Photos;
p. 14, school children, © American Stock/Archive Photos;

protest, © Archive Photos; p. 15, women workers at Radium Dial, Courtesy Argonne
National Laboratory; pp. 22-23, human brain, © George Musil; p. 24, *U.S.S. Nautilus*,
© Archive Photos; p. 24, *U.S.S. Nautilus* hat, U.S. Navy; p. 25, submarine interior,
U.S. Navy; pp. 28-29, uranium sample, © Biophoto Associates/Photo Researchers,
Inc.; p. 31, submarine, Wolfgang Bayer. All other photos
© PhotoDisc.

Illustrations: p. 5, chain reaction, Tim Alt; pp. 16-17, nuclear
power plant, Stephen Wagner.

Acknowledgments: pp. 12-13, excerpts from HIROSHIMA by
John Hersey. © 1946 by Alfred A. Knopf, a division of Random
House, Inc. Reprinted with permission.

Discovery CHANNEL SCHOOL SCIENCE

CONTENTS

NUCLEAR ENERGY

Nuclear energy—it's powerful, dangerous, and a fact of life. Once, we believed there were only four ways to transfer energy: mechanically (as in a propeller's motion), electromagnetically (as from sunlight, which helps plants to grow), chemically (as from gasoline, which mixes with air inside a combustion chamber), and heat (such as from a fire, radiator, or oven).

Now we've learned that energy is bound up as matter. It exists in the atoms of plants, propellers, car engines—everything. Some energy is bound in radioactive matter such as uranium. Once radioactive matter is transformed, it releases an incredible, staggering amount of energy. Basically, nuclear energy is matter converted to energy. But do we really know how to harness it? And what does nuclear energy mean for our future?

Nuclear energy can be terribly destructive, as the world saw when the United States dropped atomic bombs on two Japanese cities in 1945. But we have also developed ways to harness nuclear technology for other purposes, as a power source and also as a way to diagnose and battle disease. In *NUCLEAR ENERGY*, Discovery Channel takes a closer look at the origins and implications of nuclear energy, to help you decide for yourself what it means to our world.

Poised for a breakthrough.
See page 8

Final Project

3

Nuclear Energy

In 1905, German scientist Albert Einstein was trying to determine why nothing can ever go faster than the speed of light. In the course of his theorizing, Einstein began to ask about how matter and energy (such as the energy of light) are related. As he jotted down equations, he had an amazing idea. Matter and energy, he said, can be converted one into the other. The relationship can be explained by the equation $E = mc^2$. That is, energy (E) equals mass (m) times the speed of light (c) squared. The speed of light is 186,000 miles (299,274 km) per second. So if you convert mass to energy, a huge amount of energy will be released.

Fast forward. It is 1942. President Franklin Delano Roosevelt has initiated the Manhattan Project: build an atomic bomb before the Germans do, and then end the Second World War. Using Einstein's equation, a group of scientists, led by Enrico Fermi, build a nuclear reactor under a handball court at the University of Chicago. They create the first sustained nuclear reaction, converting uranium (matter) to heat (energy). At 3:25 PM on December 2, 1942, the world changed. And there was no turning back.

Nuclear energy has the power to create and destroy. The very same force that annihilated the Japanese cities of Hiroshima and Nagasaki provides energy for millions of people, lighting homes and hospitals, powering submarines, and driving new forms of medical technology. We now live with the fear of nuclear terrorism, but at the same time, we're busy building nuclear reactors with the promise of unlimited, nonpolluting energy. No other discovery in human history is so divided between unrivaled possibility and ultimate destruction. That's why learning about nuclear energy shouldn't be limited to scientists and engineers. Everyone should know all they can about this incredible power.

Physicists observe the first sustained nuclear reaction (occurring inside block structure at right) at the University of Chicago in 1942

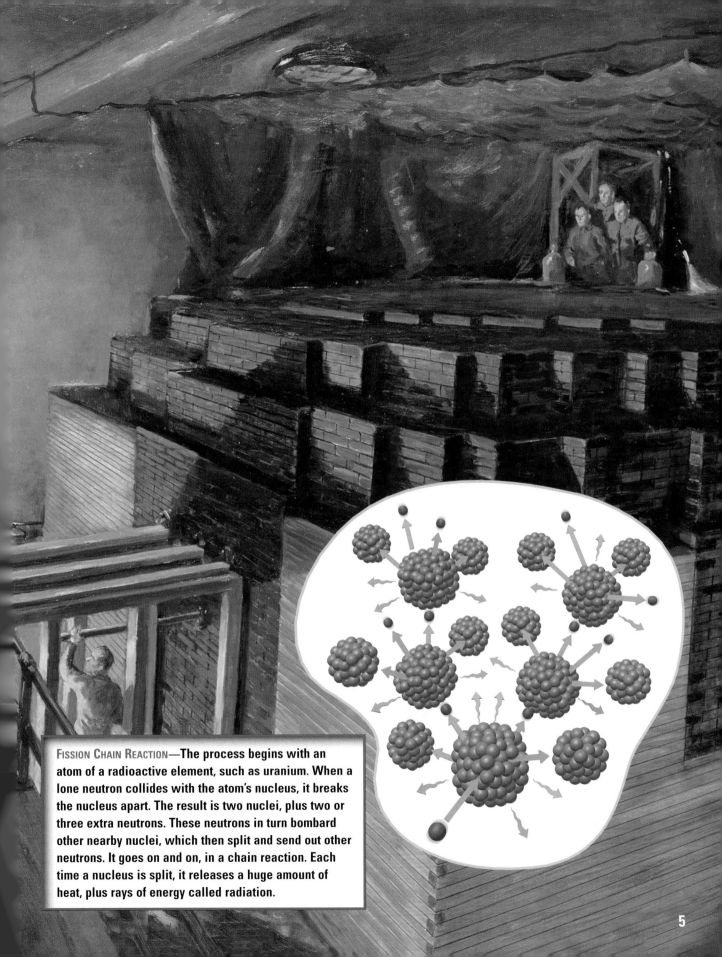

FISSION CHAIN REACTION—The process begins with an atom of a radioactive element, such as uranium. When a lone neutron collides with the atom's nucleus, it breaks the nucleus apart. The result is two nuclei, plus two or three extra neutrons. These neutrons in turn bombard other nearby nuclei, which then split and send out other neutrons. It goes on and on, in a chain reaction. Each time a nucleus is split, it releases a huge amount of heat, plus rays of energy called radiation.

Q: Our call-in show today is about nuclear energy. We've heard it's dangerous, and everyone knows what should be done with dangerous things: ban them! Caller Number One, don't you agree? Oh, and give us your name, too, please.

A: I'm the Sun. You know, that big yellow ball your planet spins around?

Q: The Sun? Why, of course! It's an honor to have such a "star" on our radio show. But why are you calling?

A: Well, I wanted to try out this new cell phone. Works great! These new telecommunications satellites sure are powerful. But the real reason I'm calling is this: I'm pretty burned up at your idea of banning nuclear energy. Plus, you can't do it.

Q: Why are you getting so hot under the collar? And what do you mean, we can't do it?

A: I mean, it's impossible to ban nuclear power production. Why, it's like banning sunshine.

Q: How so?

A: I mean, nuclear power production is a natural process. It's happening up here—right now. Where do you think my heat and light come from?

Q: Uh … something burning. Some kind of fuel. Right?

A: Right, but do you think someone hauls a big load of kindling and old newspapers up here every day and builds a fire? Besides, that kind of fire is a chemical reaction, which takes oxygen. And there's no oxygen on the Sun. Besides that, chemical reactions aren't strong enough to produce the kind of energy Earth needs. And besides THAT, I'm allergic to smoke. You want more?

Q: No, thanks—we've only got an hour. So if there's no one lighting a fire on you, how DO you keep all that heat and light coming our way? Not that we aren't grateful, mind you.

A: I'm trying to tell you: my power is made through nuclear reactions. Huge, enormous, gigantic, totally nonstop nuclear reactions go on every second in the heart of the Sun. And I don't need any fuel shipped in. It's all right here, built into my makeup, part of my mass: atoms of hydrogen.

Q: Hydrogen?! How does that turn into heat and light?

A: Nothing to it. All you need is millions of degrees of heat and millions and millions of tons of pressure—which is exactly what you'll find in my core. Under those conditions, atoms of hydrogen fuse together into a different element: helium.

Q: Well, that's all very interesting. But I still don't see what that has to do with nuclear energy, which is all about bombs and weapons.

A: Believe me, nuclear energy was around long before humans used it to make bombs and weapons. What I'm describing is a process of producing nuclear energy—a process called fusion.

Q: Wait a minute. If the process is called fusion, what does "nuclear" mean?

A: The process takes place in the center of the atoms, in a tiny particle called the nucleus. Each nucleus is made of even tinier particles called protons and neutrons. When two hydrogen nuclei meet under millions of degrees of heat and millions of tons of pressure, they come together, or fuse, into a single nucleus. This nucleus is a form of helium, but it's not your everyday helium nucleus.

Q: No? What's wrong with it?

A: It's not normal. It's unstable. It has one too many neutrons. The extra neutron escapes, and in the process a tremendous amount of heat is made. Plus

this all happens in a fraction of a second.

Q: So you start out with two nuclei and then after fusion you have only one that's been kind of welded together, plus a leftover neutron. That sounds like there's less matter left after fusion than before.

A: Yep. Every second, the Sun loses four million tons of its mass just to keep that amazing amount of energy coming your way. That's why stars like the Sun don't last forever. They're burning their own mass to make energy. And eventually they all burn out. But not to worry—I've got enough mass for several billion years more, at least.

Q: That's a relief. So—back to the bombs. Why do we call certain bombs and weapons "nuclear"?

A: Because their blasts of energy are released through a process that takes place in nuclei. Hydrogen bombs make their energy through fusion of hydrogen nuclei, just like I do. Those kinds of weapons are also called thermonuclear— "thermo" means heat. But atom bombs make their power through another nuclear process called fission. It's how nuclear power plants make energy, too.

Q: How does fission work?

A: Opposite to fusion. In fusion two nuclei fuse together. In fission, they split apart. Also, other kinds of materials are used, like plutonium or uranium. But extra neutrons escape just the same. This time, the neutrons go crashing into other nuclei, a process which breaks off more neutrons, and THEY go zooming off to break up more nuclei. That's called a chain reaction. And it produces enormous heat in a split second, just as fusion does. And it produces something else, too.

Q: What?

A: Radiation. A dangerous form of radiation is released every time fission occurs. That's why—

Q: Aha! You said dangerous! You're agreeing with me! I repeat: Nuclear energy should be banned!

A: You didn't let me finish. That's why power plants surround their reactor buildings with concrete. The concrete absorbs radiation so it doesn't get out into the atmosphere. And that's why used-up nuclear fuel is sealed and buried deep underground. But you can't ban nuclear energy. It's here to stay. Believe me—I ought to know.

Activity

LIGHTEN UP! We use several different forms of energy, including nuclear power, to generate electricity. Each method has its own benefits, disadvantages, and degree of risk to the community. Find out about several different sources for energy, and compare the methods each uses to prevent accidents and keep workers safe. Investigate hydroelectricity, wind energy, solar energy, and nuclear energy.

Chain Reaction

Marie Curie in her lab

1896–1911	1932	1934–1939	1942–1945	1949–1953

REVELATIONS

French physicist Antoine Henri Becquerel discovers that the element uranium gives off energy in the form of invisible rays. In 1898, Marie and Pierre Curie find other elements that produce radiation. British physicist Ernest Rutherford discovers two kinds of radioactive rays, which he calls alpha and beta rays. These are later found to be high-energy particles. In 1911, Rutherford discovers the nucleus of the atom. A new branch of science is born: nuclear physics.

SHOTS IN THE DARK

Two German radiochemists, Otto Hahn and Fritz Strassman, bombard uranium with neutron particles and produce the first artificial fission reaction. Because the reaction produces more energy than it consumes, scientists realize that fission has the potential to release a tremendous amount of energy. The exact amount can be calculated from Albert Einstein's theory of relativity (developed in 1905): $E=mc^2$. This understanding is the basis for the creation of nuclear bombs and nuclear power.

RADIATION FIGHTS CANCER

The discovery of artificial radiation by Irène Juliot-Curie and her husband Jean-Frédéric Juliot leads to the development of radiotherapy as a treatment for cancer.

WAR BREAKS OUT

German-born physicist Albert Einstein writes a letter to President Franklin Roosevelt. He explains that it might be possible to make an atomic bomb and urges Roosevelt to fund U.S. research. Einstein suspects that Nazi Germany is already studying the release of nuclear energy, and he fears that the Germans might come up with a bomb first. A month later, the Second World War is underway.

TOP SECRET

Physicist Enrico Fermi and his colleagues at the University of Chicago create the first artificial nuclear chain reaction on December 2, 1942. Some of the world's best scientific minds—Fermi, J. Robert Oppenheimer, Albert Einstein, Leo Szilard, and others—spend the next few years working to develop an atomic bomb for the U.S. The project's code name is "the Manhattan Project."

BRIGHTER THAN 1,000 SUNS

On July 16, 1945, in the desert near Alamagordo, New Mexico, the scientists of the Manhattan Project successfully conduct the world's first nuclear test. Less than a month later, the U.S. drops two atomic bombs on Japan. The bombs kill more than 130,000 people. Thousands more later die from radiation sickness.

THE ARMS RACE

In 1949, the Soviet Union succeeds in creating an atomic bomb. In 1952, the U.S. tests the first hydrogen bomb. It's a thousand times more powerful than the bombs dropped on Hiroshima and Nagasaki. The Soviets test their own hydrogen bomb in 1953. In the years that follow, France, China, the United Kingdom, and India all explode nuclear bombs in tests.

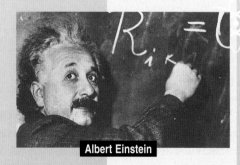

Albert Einstein

J. Robert Oppenheimer

Atomic bomb blast

The discovery of nuclear energy in the twentieth century was a turning point for science and for humanity. The greatest advances took place before and during World War II, building up to the development of the atomic bomb. For the first time, humans had the power to destroy much of life on Earth.

Yet people understood that nuclear energy could also be harnessed for other uses that were not purely destructive. Soon after the war, nuclear technology was developed as a power source, mainly to provide electricity. As more and more power plants were built, it became clear that there were new dangers and risks to take into account. Disposing of harmful radioactive waste was a threat to the environment. And several major accidents at nuclear power plants around the world raised the critical question: Is nuclear energy worth the risks?

1950s	1957–1970s	1970s–1980s	1990s	1999, 2000, 2001...

ATOMS FOR PEACE

U.S. President Dwight Eisenhower creates the Atoms for Peace program, an international group devoted to developing peaceful uses for nuclear power. His goal is to take nuclear power "out of the hands of soldiers" and adapt it "to the arts of peace." Today, electric power production is the most widely used application of nuclear energy for nonmilitary purposes.

NUKES AT WORK

In 1957, the first full-scale nuclear power plant in the U.S. begins generating electricity in Shippingport, PA. The United Nations establishes the International Atomic Energy Agency to promote the peaceful use of nuclear energy, and the European Atomic Energy Community is formed to encourage the development of nuclear power. During the 1960s and 1970s, many countries build nuclear reactors. Progress is also made toward limiting nuclear weapons testing and stopping the spread of nuclear weapons.

MELTDOWN

People grow more aware of the risks nuclear energy poses to the environment and humans. In 1979, equipment failures and human error at Three Mile Island nuclear power plant near Harrisburg, PA, releases poisonous radioactive gases into the air. In 1986, the Chernobyl nuclear power plant, near Kiev, Russia, has a worse accident. Thirty-one people are killed and 75 million are exposed to dangerously high levels of radiation. The long-term damage won't be assessed for years to come.

DEVELOPMENT OF NUCLEAR RADIOLOGY

Diagnostic equipment using nuclear technology gains wider use in the medical field. The procedure uses radioactive material which, when injected or swallowed, sends signals to sensitive equipment, such as PET scanners. These machines produce images, allowing doctors to study possible internal disorders without needing to perform exploratory surgery.

TODAY AND TOMORROW

A major incident takes place in September, 1999, outside of Tokyo, Japan. More than 50 people receive dangerously high doses of radiation, and residents of the area are told to stay indoors. Despite the risks and concerns, more than 425 nuclear power plants operate in over 30 countries. Nuclear energy is recognized as a relatively cheap alternative to traditional sources of energy, and safety remains a key issue.

Dwight Eisenhower

Enrico Fermi

Activity

WHAT IF? Dr. Enrico Fermi was an Italian. When Fermi was awarded the Nobel Prize in 1938, Fascist dictator Benito Mussolini ruled Italy. The Fascist government allowed Fermi to leave the country so that he could receive the award in Sweden. Instead of returning, he and his family moved to America. Find out more about Fermi's contribution to the development of nuclear energy. How might history have been different if he hadn't managed to leave Italy? How might World War II have turned out? Using this scenario, write your own hypothetical timeline of the war and its aftermath.

The Light Stuff

Many scientists of the early 20th century spent their days in labs, conducting experiments. Not Albert Einstein. He did some of his best scientific work while taking a stroll. As he walked, he pondered the realities of the physical world. "The whole of science," he said, "is nothing more than a refinement of everyday thinking."

Born in Germany, Einstein settled in Bern, Switzerland, in 1902. He was trained as a physicist but wasn't able to get a job teaching. To support his family, Einstein worked in the Swiss patent office. In his free moments, Einstein focused his thoughts on science.

Einstein was extraordinarily brilliant. He enjoyed probing the notions of space, time, and, especially, light. Einstein was also something of a rebel; he was quick to question the so-called "truths" he learned in school if they didn't mesh with his own thoughts of what was logical and true.

Science in Revolt

This questioning of accepted wisdom led Einstein to his greatest discoveries. At the turn of the 19th century, some physicists were conducting experiments that challenged the old system of physics. These experiments led to new theories, which helped Einstein shape his own theories of the nature of the world.

The old physics were dominated by Sir Isaac Newton (1642–1727), an English scientist. Newon's ideas dealt primarily with the motion of objects and the force of gravity. In Newton's physics, time and space were always absolute, or fixed.

While still in his teens, Einstein puzzled over Newton's idea about absolutes of time and space and how they relate to light. By then, scientists knew the speed of light: 186,000 (1.86×10^5) miles (299,274 km) per second. Einstein considered this information and took it a step further: What would happen if he could run along a light wave and match its speed?

A Special Theory

Einstein continued to grapple with this problem while working at the Swiss patent office. One of his finest accomplishments was to suggest that time and space were relative, not absolute.

Einstein's theory came together in fragments. He strolled alone through the nearby countryside, lost in his thoughts. He discussed them with his friend Michele Angelo Besso as the two men walked the streets of Bern. One day in the spring of 1905, Einstein told Besso he was ready to throw away the whole theory— he just couldn't make it work.

When Einstein woke up the next day, he was jolted by a clarity of thought. "A storm broke loose in my head," he later said. He began to write down his Theory of Special Relativity—special because it dealt only with objects that move at a constant speed relative to each other. (A Theory of General Relativity followed ten years later.) The only fixed, absolute calculation in Einstein's theory was the speed of light. But, Einstein said, everything else—time, speed, space—were relative to the motion of the person observing them.

Years after devising his theory, Einstein came up with a lighthearted definition of relativity: "When you are courting a nice girl, an hour seems like a second. When you sit on a red hot cinder, a second seems like an hour."

Three Famous Letters

To fully understand relativity, Einstein applied his theory to the relation between light, energy, and the mass of objects. He concluded that an object's mass represented a special condition of energy, and energy is a special condition of mass. Einstein came up with a formula to express the relationship between energy and mass: $E=mc^2$. "E" represents energy, "m" stands for mass, and "c^2" is the speed of light multiplied by itself. The formula looked simple enough—until scientists began to consider what it really meant. The tiniest amount of matter contained enormous quantities of energy. One unit of mass equals 34.6 billion units of energy (34.6×10^{10}).

Einstein posed a question: How could so much energy stored inside the tiniest atom never have been noticed before? "The answer is simple enough," he said, "so long as none of the energy is given off externally, it cannot be observed. It is as though a man who is fabulously rich should never spend or give away a cent; no one could tell how rich he was."

In the years after Einstein created his famous formula, scientists explored ways to unlock the energy stored inside atoms. Splitting an atom apart, a process called fission, unleashed the energy inside. The original atom became two smaller atoms; their total mass was less than the mass of the original atom. The rest of the first atom's mass was released as energy.

In 1939, Germany was run by Adolf Hitler and the country was preparing to launch a war in Europe. Einstein and other physicists feared that the Germans would find a way to harness atomic energy in a terribly destructive new bomb. Einstein, now living in America, wrote President Franklin Roosevelt, warning of the dangers and calling for the United States to begin its own atomic weapons research.

Einstein didn't see himself as the "father" of atomic energy. But his formula and the research it sparked led to nuclear fission and a new source for electrical power. It also led to nuclear weapons, which Einstein called a "menace" that could lead to "unparalleled catastrophes."

Brain Gain

When Albert Einstein died in 1955, his brain was removed for scientific study. Since then, three reports have come out describing how Einstein's brain compared to the brains of "normal" people (folks who aren't scientific geniuses). Some of the conclusions:

- The density of certain cells in his brain was higher than normal.
- The part of the brain used for scientific and mathematical reasoning seemed to be larger than average.

Activity

THINK IT THROUGH Think of something you do every day: flush a toilet, ride a bike, play a video game, talk on the phone. Come up with ways to improve that activity. You don't have to be an Einstein, you just have to think it through.

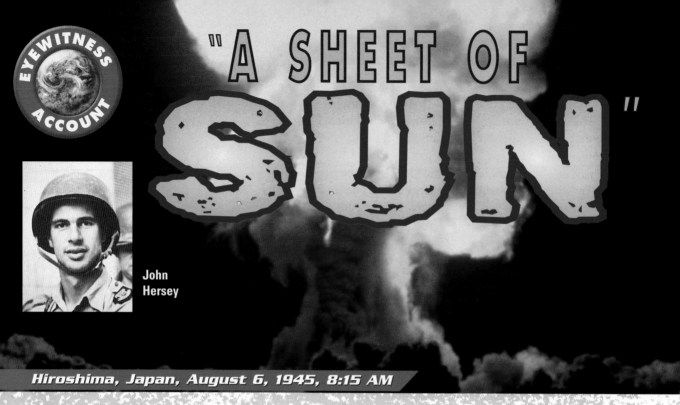

"A SHEET OF SUN"

John Hersey

Hiroshima, Japan, August 6, 1945, 8:15 AM

A single American B-29 bomber, the *Enola Gay*, flew over the Japanese city of Hiroshima and dropped an atomic bomb. The explosion was the equivalent of 12,500 tons of TNT. The city was flattened in a matter of seconds. Of a total population of about 245,000, more than 100,000 were killed immediately. Another 100,000 were injured, and, in just a few months, thousands more would die from radiation sickness, injuries, and other ailments related to the blast.

The Enola Gay

Three days later, the United States dropped another bomb on Nagasaki, and Japan surrendered. World War II was finally over.

Why was this devastating action taken? Although the Allies had won the war in Europe, the fighting in the Pacific continued to drag on, with no end in sight. Japan, though weakened, resorted to ever more desperate tactics to hold back a U.S. invasion, sinking ships and killing thousands of crew members with each offensive. The Allies presented Japan with an ultimatum on July 26, 1945, which was ignored. It came down to a choice between ending the war immediately, or suffering more and more casualties—on both sides—until Japan finally decided to give in. U.S. president Harry Truman and his advisors chose the immediate action, but no one predicted the magnitude of the destruction unleashed by the bomb.

Not long after the blast, John Hersey, a young war reporter, went to Hiroshima and interviewed many of the survivors. Their accounts were published the following year. Americans realized that the bomb wasn't simply a weapon used against their mortal enemies across the Pacific, but a disaster that struck ordinary civilians, fathers and mothers, priests, doctors, and soldiers—in other words, people just like them.

A Noiseless Flash

Mr. Tanimoto and Mr. Matsuo were delivering a heavy cabinet to an estate in Koi, a residential district outside of the city.

Then a tremendous flash of light cut across the sky. Mr. Tanimoto has a distinct recollection that it traveled from east to west, from the city toward the hills. It seemed a sheet of sun. Both he and Mr. Matsuo reacted in terror. . . . Mr. Matsuo dashed up the front steps into the house and dived among the bedrolls and buried himself there. Mr. Tanimoto took four or five steps and threw himself between two big

rocks in the garden. . . . He felt a sudden pressure, and then splinters and pieces of board and fragments of tile fell on him. He heard no roar.

Tower of Dust, Heat, and Fission

The survivors observed strange atmospheric effects from the bomb. Mr. Tanimoto gazed at the ruined city:

Clumps of smoke, near and far, had begun to push up through the general dust. He wondered how such extensive damage could have been dealt out of a silent sky; even a few planes, far up, would have been audible. Houses nearby were burning, and when huge drops of water the size of marbles began to fall, he half thought that they must be coming from the hoses of firemen fighting the blazes. (They were actually drops of condensed moisture falling from the turbulent tower of dust, heat, and fission fragments that had already risen miles into the sky above Hiroshima.)

What had once been a prosperous urban center was now little more than rubble. Father Kleinsorge, a Jesuit priest, went back into the city twelve days after the explosion.

By now he was accustomed to the terrible scene: . . . the houses on the outskirts of the city, standing but decrepit, with broken windows and disheveled tiles; and then, quite suddenly, the beginning of the four square miles of reddish-brown scar, where nearly everything had been buffeted down and burned; range on range of collapsed city blocks, with here and there a crude sign erected on a pile of ashes and tiles ("Sister, where are you?" or "All safe and we live at Toyosaka"); naked trees and canted telephone poles . . . and in the streets a macabre traffic—hundreds of crumpled bicycles, shells of streetcars and automobiles, all halted in mid-motion. The whole way, Father Kleinsorge was oppressed by the thought that all the damage he saw had been done in one instant by one bomb.

Activity

FINDING PRECEDENTS The Second World War was the first major conflict in which many people—soldiers and civilians alike—were killed in large numbers from bombardments. Unfortunately, the terrible statistics of the atomic bombs at Hiroshima and Nagasaki were not unique. Research other major bombardments of the war, including the London Blitz, Pearl Harbor, Hamburg, Dresden, and Tokyo, and compare the numbers of people killed and injured. What aspects of each bombardment caused the most damage? How did the bombs themselves compare, in terms of quantity and how destructive they were? Put your results in a chart, and include the date of each bombardment. Draw one or two major conclusions from your data about the use of bombs in warfare.

Fear of Fallout

Air Raid Drill

At first, people were excited about the possibilities and implications of nuclear energy. We had discovered that atoms could do things never before imagined! Inventors came up with all kinds of ideas for making a profit off the new technology. But it didn't take long for people to catch on that radiation was also extremely dangerous. The atomic weapons buildup that followed World War II only made things worse in people's imaginations. If the nations couldn't hold back in making more and more destructive weapons, did that mean the world would soon come to an end?

During the 1950s and 1960s, schools held "duck and cover" drills to prepare children for a nuclear attack. Kids hid under their desks and covered their heads, or kneeled against the wall with their heads between their knees and hands over their faces. They were told to stay in position until an "all-clear" siren sounded. In a real nuclear attack, these precautions wouldn't do much good. The kids might be safe from shards of glass and other debris, but not from the harmful effects of radiation.

Miracle Cure... Not!

In the 1920s, a businessman by the name of William J. A. Bailey concocted a "remedy" called Radithor. The key ingredient was a radioactive element called radium. Bailey claimed that this medicine would make people younger and healthier, and many people believed him. After drinking Radithor faithfully for five years, a prominent Pittsburgh citizen, Eben Byers, died of radiation poisoning. This was the first proven death resulting from a radioactive medicine. The incident received a lot of publicity but, at the same time, doctors were developing ways to use radiation safely, especially in the treatment of cancer.

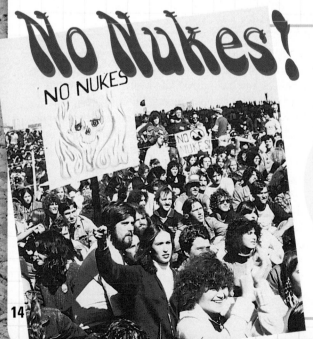

No Nukes!

In the late 1960s, many people began to doubt the wisdom and safety of nuclear power. Organizations like Greenpeace were formed to protest weapons testing and the dumping of radioactive nuclear waste. Large-scale protests and fund-raising concerts were organized in the 1970s by MUSE (standing for "Musicians United for Safe Energy") to inform people about alternative energy sources. One of their protest songs included these lyrics:

Give me the warm power of the sun,
Give me the steady flow of the waterfall,
Give me the restless power of the wind—
But take all your atomic, poison power away.

Shelter From The Storm

Ever wonder what those signs that say "Fallout Shelter" really mean? "Fallout" is highly radioactive debris that would be floating around in the air following a nuclear explosion. In 1961, the U.S. Office of Civilian Defense Mobilization began a public fallout shelter program to protect Americans in the event of a nuclear attack. Various underground locations were designated as civil defense shelters and marked with yellow and black signs. Many shelters were set up in the basements of apartment and office buildings, factories, schools, and other large structures, or in windowless central areas in buildings above ground.

Many people in the 1950s and 1960s spent large sums of money building their own private fallout shelters in their backyards. But let's face it: How long could you live cramped underground? Critics pointed out that there would never be enough safe shelter space for everyone. Novels and films about nuclear catastrophes showed neighbors fighting each other at shelter entrances. And what would happen when it was safe to come out? If a hydrogen bomb were dropped, fire and heat from the blast would be a more immediate problem than fallout. And radioactive particles would remain in the atmosphere for years to come.

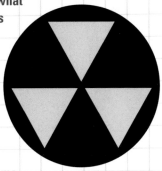

Chicago, Illinois, 1938

FORMER WORKER WINS SETTLEMENT

Catherine Wolfe Donahue was awarded a cash settlement from Radium Dial Company today. She was one of several workers to take the company to court after becoming gravely ill from the effects of radiation poisoning.

Donahue was so ill, in fact, that she had to be carried from the courtroom after the suit was settled. When her health first began to fail after she started working at Radium Dial several years ago, doctors suspected anemia. Now the diagnosis may be a type of cancer.

Workers at Radium Dial used radium-based paint to decorate the surfaces of glow-in-the-dark watches that recently became popular. To get a fine enough point for drawing the numbers on such a small surface, the workers, many of them young women, licked their paintbrushes.

What the workers didn't know was that for many of them, radium was collecting in their teeth and bones. Workers were tested for radioactivity but not informed of their condition. The results of the physical exams were revealed publicly in the course of the lawsuit against Radium Dial. Many other workers have since fallen ill, and some have died from the radiation poisoning.

Glow-in-the-Dark Today

These days, glow-in-the-dark effects are produced not from radioactive paint, but from substances that glow (phosphoresce) simply by being exposed to light.

Whaat goes on inside a nuclear power plant? Perhaps you've seen those funny-looking, curved cylinders. These are the cooling towers. But there's a lot more to a nuclear power plant—let's take a look inside to see how the pieces work together.

Nuclear power plants generate electricity by harnessing the energy created during nuclear fission. The energy from fission is released as heat: this is used to boil water, creating steam. This steam turns a turbine, which generates electricity. A nuclear power plant actually involves several different kinds of energy transfer: nuclear energy produces heat energy, which produces steam, whose mechanical energy turns a generator. And the generator produces energy in the form of electricity.

Instant Reaction

The nuclear reactor is where the main action takes place. The energy the reactor releases is in the form of heat. The reactor core, or pressure vessel, is where the fuel does its work. The pressure vessel is cased in thick concrete and a larger structure of steel to shield the outside world from the dangerous radioactive materials inside the core.

Hot Rods

The fuel for a nuclear power plant is in the form of small pellets of a specially-enriched, radioactive material called uranium oxide. These pellets are inserted in metal tubes that are about 12 to 14 feet long (3–4 m) and less than 1 inch (2.5 cm) in diameter. The tubes are bundled together and put into the reactor core. A typical nuclear power plant has about 50,000 of these fuel rods, which altogether hold about 100 tons of uranium. Make no mistake—these fuel rods are hot. Try about 570°F (299°C). This heat is generated by the nuclear fission taking place within the rods.

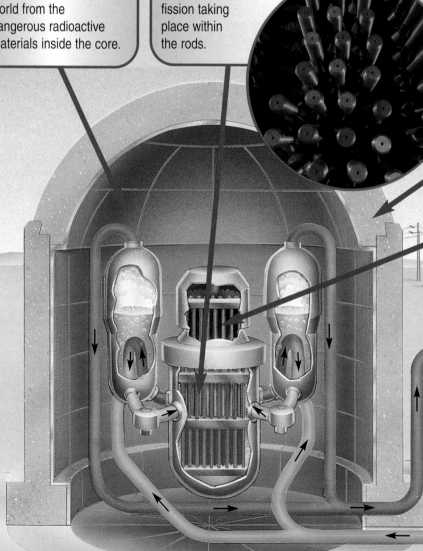

Cool Down

On the Outside

A nuclear power plant must be built to keep the radioactive matter from escaping to the outside environment. So the dome-shaped housing for the reactor is made of thick concrete lined with steel, which radioactivity can't penetrate. The buildings also have to be solid enough to prevent accidents from outside intruding in. The structure around the reactor, for example, is strong enough to withstand a collision with a jetliner!

Hold Your Horses

Hot is good—to a point. The reactor needs to be hot if it's going to do its job. But if it gets too hot, there's trouble. If the rate of nuclear fission gets out of control, the temperature rises to the point where the uranium itself could melt. It can also melt through the metal rods and concrete housing, releasing dangerous radioactive materials into the ground or air around the power station. Another word for this is "meltdown." Control rods help prevent meltdowns when they are positioned among the bundles of fuel rods inside the reactor. The control rods control the rate of fission reactions as they are constantly being lowered into and raised out of the fuel assemblies inside the reactor.

Water, Water Everywhere

Water flows into the reactor core, all around the fuel rods, and out again. Water works as a coolant, to prevent the reactor from getting too hot. It also gets boiling hot and converts to steam. This steam travels outside the pressure vessel and turns a system of high-pressure turbines. These, in turn, spin a generator. And the generator produces power, just as your average coal-fueled power plant does. The steam, meanwhile, is converted back to water in one of these giant vase-shaped cooling towers.

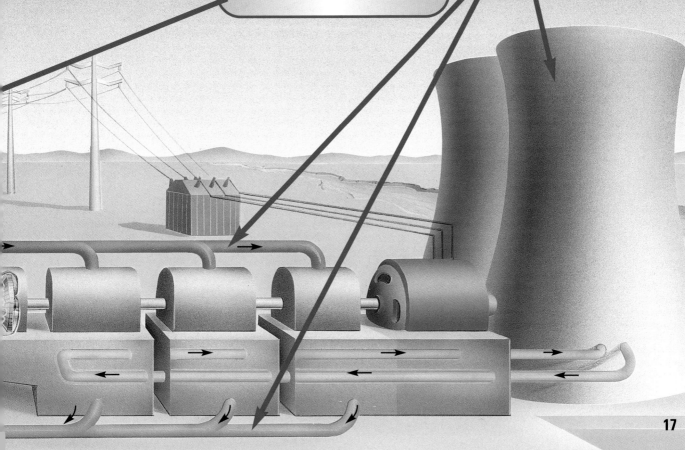

Caution! May Be Harmful to Your Health

Radiation! It sounds scary, but in basic terms radiation is energy in the form of various small, moving particles. And radiation can be useful: Radiowaves and microwaves are forms of radiation. Nuclear medicine uses radiation to detect and treat certain diseases, such as cancer. And radiation exists in nature, coming from trees and rocks. It's even produced inside you, by potassium in your blood.

But one kind of radiation, called ionizing radiation, can be dangerous, especially in high doses. Ionizing radiation is released during the production of nuclear energy. Inside the body, ionizing radiation damages or kills cells. This damage can lead to cancer. Large doses of radiation can destroy the body's organs, an illness called radiation sickness. If the cells used for reproduction are damaged, radiation can also cause birth defects.

There are three major types of ionizing radiation:

Alpha particles — dangerous if inhaled or taken into the body on food; can be stopped by a piece of paper or a layer of human skin

Beta particles — can enter the body but will eventually stop penetrating; also dangerous if inhaled or eaten; can be stopped by a thin sheet of aluminum foil

Gamma rays — easily pass through the body, possibly damaging organs; can be stopped by a few inches of lead, a few feet of concrete, or deep pools of water

Alpha particles
Beta particles
Gamma rays

paper · aluminum foil · concrete

Measuring Up

Radiation is measured in units called rems and millirems (that's 1/1,000th of a rem). Check out the rems of radiation around you—and find out how much is too much.

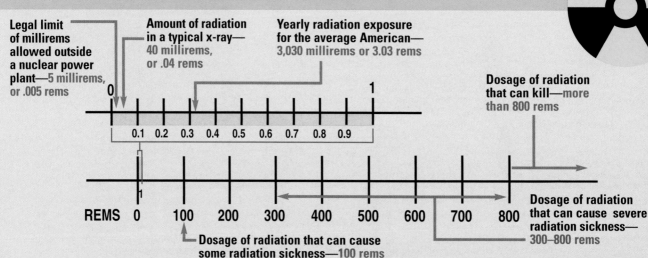

Legal limit of millirems allowed outside a nuclear power plant—5 millirems, or .005 rems

Amount of radiation in a typical x-ray—40 millirems, or .04 rems

Yearly radiation exposure for the average American—3,030 millirems or 3.03 rems

Dosage of radiation that can kill—more than 800 rems

0   0.1 0.2 0.3 0.4 0.5 0.6 0.7 0.8 0.9   1

REMS   0   100   200   300   400   500   600   700   800

Dosage of radiation that can cause some radiation sickness—100 rems

Dosage of radiation that can cause severe radiation sickness—300–800 rems

NO HOMERS ALLOWED

It may be funny in a cartoon to see Homer Simpson goofing off and napping on his job at a nuclear power plant, but Homer wouldn't last twenty minutes at a real nuclear plant. According to Victor Dricks of the Nuclear Regulatory Commission, reactor staffers have to pass difficult tests to be hired, and they are constantly updating their training. All the work they do is subject to double and triple checks, and there is a government inspector assigned full time to every one of the 109 nuclear power plants in the United States. Nuclear safety guidelines were overhauled and tightened after the Three Mile Island accident in 1979. "All of the plants now coach each other on how to improve safety performance," Dricks said. "There's been a dramatic effect: In the twenty years since Three-Mile Island, there have been no serious accidents."

fission fashion Note "Despite what you see in the movies, most nuclear reactor staff members dress casually," says Dricks. When protective clothing is required — such as when maintenance or repairs are underway— workers wear cotton jumpsuits, respirators to breathe through, and rubber booties. They carry machines called dosimeters to measure their radiation exposure, which is carefully tracked annually and kept within set limits.

Get a Half-Life

The radiation in elements can take a long time to lose its deadly power. Scientists talk about an element's half-life—how long it takes for one-half of a certain amount of the element to be safe. Here's an example: one kind of uranium has a half-life of about 700 million years. Take a one-pound piece of this uranium. After 700 million years, a half-pound of it would still be radioactive. Another 700 million years later, a quarter-pound would still be radioactive.

Why is the half-life of radioactive elements important? Because nuclear plants create nuclear waste, and this waste will remain radioactive for many thousands of years. One of the gravest safety issues with nuclear power is finding a reliable way to contain the radiation from the waste. In the past, waste buried underground has leaked out of its containers and contaminated nearby soil and water. Cleaning up the leaks exposed workers to radiation. There's a danger such leaks could also contaminate people who live near the waste sites.

What a Waste

Anything that comes in contact with radiation can be contaminated, so it must be safely stored far away from populated communities. Even the materials used to contain and transport waste become nuclear waste.

Type of Waste
Low Level Waste that has low levels of radiation and does not need special shielding during transport. Includes tools used in uranium mining, clothing worn by nuclear workers, and lab equipment. Disposal: Placed in steel drums and buried up to 20 feet (6 m). Drums sometimes covered with concrete shells.
Intermediate Level Products that are about one thousand times more radioactive than low-level waste. Requires special shielding during transport. Includes the cans used to hold uranium fuel for nuclear power plants. Disposal: Deeper burial in the ground than low-level waste.
High Level Most radioactive, with half-life of tens of thousands of years. Includes used uranium fuel rods. Rods must be cooled and stored in water before they are moved. Disposal: Currently fuel rods are kept on the site where they were used. The U.S. government is exploring a site in Nevada for permanent storage of high-level waste.

Activity

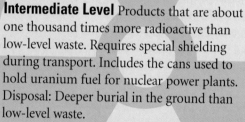

FAST REACTION In nuclear fission, an atom splits in two. Particles then collide with other atoms, splitting them, and so on. This continues through what is called a chain reaction. To see how quickly a chain reaction occurs, take a calculator and input the number 2. Multiply that number by 2. Repeat three more times. How many atom collisions have occurred? Suppose that on average atoms collide every second. How many collisions will there be after 30 seconds? After a minute?

The Powers That Be

Did you know that the United States has more nuclear reactors in operation than any other nation in the world? But the 109 reactors in the United States provide less than 20 percent of the energy we use. By contrast, Lithuania has only two reactors—but they provide 77 percent of its energy. Compare some of the countries shown on this map. You'll see which ones rely heavily on nuclear power, and which get more of their energy from fossil fuels, such as oil, coal, and gasoline.

Key of Chart Headings

Number of nuclear reactors	Percentage of energy from nuclear power	Percentage of energy from fossil fuels

CANADA

UNITED STATES

MEXICO

BRAZIL

ARGENTINA

North and South America

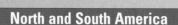

Country			OIL
Argentina	2	10	45
Brazil	1	1	4
Canada	14	12	20
Mexico	2	5	71
USA	109	19	65

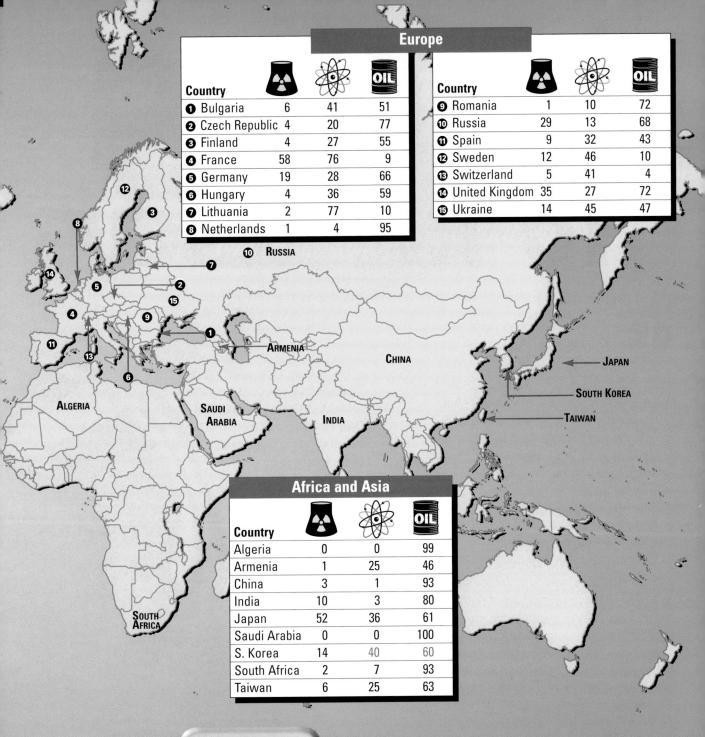

Europe

Country	☢	⚛	OIL
❶ Bulgaria	6	41	51
❷ Czech Republic	4	20	77
❸ Finland	4	27	55
❹ France	58	76	9
❺ Germany	19	28	66
❻ Hungary	4	36	59
❼ Lithuania	2	77	10
❽ Netherlands	1	4	95

Country	☢	⚛	OIL
❾ Romania	1	10	72
❿ Russia	29	13	68
⓫ Spain	9	32	43
⓬ Sweden	12	46	10
⓭ Switzerland	5	41	4
⓮ United Kingdom	35	27	72
⓯ Ukraine	14	45	47

Africa and Asia

Country	☢	⚛	OIL
Algeria	0	0	99
Armenia	1	25	46
China	3	1	93
India	10	3	80
Japan	52	36	61
Saudi Arabia	0	0	100
S. Korea	14	40	60
South Africa	2	7	93
Taiwan	6	25	63

Activity

BY THE NUMBERS What parts of the world use very little nuclear energy compared to other types of energy? What parts use a great deal? Choose three nations from three different parts of the world, and find out how heavily they rely on (a) fossil fuels; (b) hydroelectricity; (c) wind and solar power; and (d) nuclear power. Display this information as percentages, in a pie chart, so you can see how the countries compare in their energy uses. Consider the following issues: location of fossil fuel reserves; global climate; topography; tides and rivers. What conclusions can you draw for each country about the factors that influence the use of nuclear power?

RAYS
TO THE RESCUE

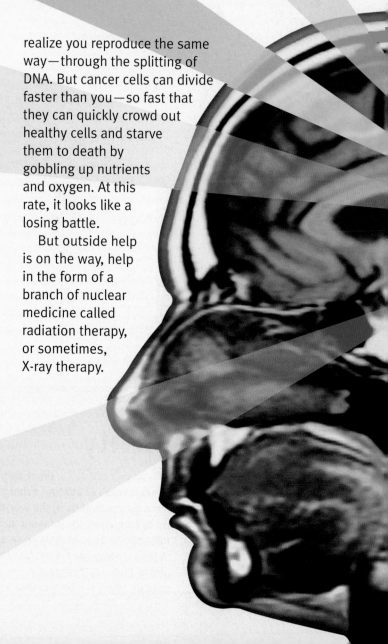

Imagine you're small. Now imagine you're smaller. Keep going. Smaller, smaller . . . that's it. Now you're microscopic. Small enough to get under someone's skin. Literally. And now suddenly you've become a healthy human nerve cell. You're long, pale, stringlike, and you reside in a human brain— one tiny link in the superhighway along which electrical impulses travel, carrying messages to and from other parts of the body.

You've been drafted to fight a war going on inside the body. Winning it won't be easy. Your attackers have certain cell superpowers and even as you watch, their numbers are growing. They're multiplying, ganging up, massing into a huge cluster. Your enemy is a tumor—a cancerous tumor. This tumor has been declared inoperable—too big, and in too dangerous a place to risk surgical removal.

You are located close enough to observe the tumor but you're not on the actual front line. You notice that even though you and a cancer cell are bitter enemies, you do have something in common: You both have a center called a nucleus, which contains genetic material, or DNA. You watch a cancer cell reproduce, divide into two cells, and you realize you reproduce the same way—through the splitting of DNA. But cancer cells can divide faster than you—so fast that they can quickly crowd out healthy cells and starve them to death by gobbling up nutrients and oxygen. At this rate, it looks like a losing battle.

But outside help is on the way, help in the form of a branch of nuclear medicine called radiation therapy, or sometimes, X-ray therapy.

This treatment uses high-energy beams of light to break down cancer cells so they can't reproduce. The beams' energy is so intense that the cancerous cells are broken apart into chemically reactive particles called ions.

The treatment begins. It's called teletherapy, long-distance therapy, and it uses an external source of radiation. The beam passes through you, penetrating bone, deep into the brain. But you receive no pain messages, and you stay intact. Radiation therapy is painless—but effective. You feel unchanged, but after several hours you notice a change in the cancer cells. The ones in the middle of the tumor look dead. They've stopped dividing. They've gathered into a pool of liquid.

Looks as if the first battle is over—but the war is far from won. The center may be dead, but the cells around the edges, close to the blood vessels, are continuing their high-speed division and growth. Red blood cells contain oxygen and the cancer cells are eagerly absorbing it. But they'll soon be sorry. The more oxygen in a cell, the more damage radiation can cause.

The next day, more high-energy beams pass through you. You're still fine. One of your chromosomes is broken, but you are able to repair it yourself.

The days pass with more and more rays and now it's definite: the mass is shrinking. As the cancer cells pass through their cycle of sensitivity, they become more and more harmed by the radiation. It's called selective damage, and it is one of the goals of radiation therapy.

So why are *you* still alive? Because you have a greater tolerance for the treatment. And also because the therapy was planned to occur over time. One large dose would have killed both healthy and cancer cells alike. Another reason is that once the first few treatments shrunk the tumor, it left more nutrients and oxygen available for surviving cells.

Some healthy cells right around the tumor have been destroyed. But many more have survived. And the tumor is now small enough to be removed by surgery, with much less risk of accidentally causing paralysis or other problems. You've just witnessed how radiation can be harnessed to save countless lives.

Activity

X MARKS THE SPOT X-rays are a type of electromagnetic radiation that occurs naturally in the light we get from the Sun. In 1895, German physicist Wilhelm Conrad Röntgen discovered their existence and named them "X-rays" because of their unknown origin. In 1903, surgeon Georg Clems Perthes discovered that X-rays inhibit the growth of cancer cells. Learn more about these men and how the use of X-rays helps in detecting everything from cavities in your teeth to tumors in your lungs.

Underwater and

A new vessel has just been launched, and there it goes, moving sleekly down the Thames River in Connecticut towards the Atlantic Ocean. The world has never seen anything like it before. They're saying it can go for months and months without ever having to refuel. What the heck is it?

It's a nuclear-powered submarine, that's what!

Until the 1950s, submarines were driven using standard methods. Diesel engines powered them when they traveled above the surface of the water, and electric batteries took over when they went below. Unfortunately, this system had several drawbacks. For one thing, submarine batteries lost power very quickly. A submarine could stay under water only as long as its battery could hold out— perhaps three or four days if the sub drifted with the current, a few hours if it went at top speed. After that, the sub needed to surface and recharge the battery.

A second problem involved the fuel burned by the diesel engines. The fuel took up lots of room and its weight slowed down the ship. It also burned quickly. Submarines were constantly taking time out to refuel. For years, naval officials and scientists alike worked on this problem: The weight and capacity of its power systems seriously limited what the sub could do.

A Breakthrough Idea

Enter the U. S. Navy's Hyman Rickover. Captain Rickover was a man of big ideas, and perhaps his biggest idea of all involved nuclear energy. In Rickover's plan, every submarine would exchange diesel engines and batteries for a small nuclear reactor. Instead of burning oil, the reactor would split uranium atoms. The atoms would produce heat, which could be used to power the submarine.

Rickover's idea made good sense. Nuclear energy had two huge advantages over coal, oil, and batteries. First, it was much more powerful. Second, creating and storing nuclear energy used little space and added little weight. That combination made it possible to pack an enormous amount of fuel into a very small area—a big plus in a submarine with little elbow room! A nuclear submarine would be able to cruise underwater for weeks, even months, without resurfacing.

The next step was to build a working nuclear sub. Rickover and his workers created the *Nautilus*, the world's first nuclear submarine. Once it was launched in 1954, the *Nautilus* proved to be exactly as advertised. On one early voyage, the sub cruised for two years without refueling. Today, nuclear subs make up the bulk of submarines in the largest navies of the world. They can travel 400,000 miles (643,600 km) before replacing the uranium in their reactors, and they may spend up to four months almost entirely underwater.

In many ways, a nuclear-powered submarine is like a small town, complete with modern conveniences. Hot water, excellent food, air conditioning, a library, a movie theater showing the latest releases, a state-of-the-art sound system . . . and it's a good thing, too. Imagine being in a small vessel underwater for four months or more. Without a doubt, the crews of these fully-supplied "floating towns" need the stimulation of all these special features, or they would miss the outside world too much.

Out in Space

Out of Orbit

The success of nuclear-powered submarines has led many researchers to think about building nuclear-powered rockets. As was once the case with submarines, spaceship fuel is enormously heavy. In fact, most of the weight of a space mission consists of fuel and engine. That extra weight drastically limits the speed and range of a spacecraft. With conventional fuels, a trip to Saturn would take about seven years—and you could forget about getting home again. Even a round trip to nearby Mars could take two years. If you left home as a seventh grader, you'd be old enough for high school when you got back to Earth.

But nuclear energy could change all that. Atomic fuel can propel a rocket with much more force than conventional methods allow. Cutting down on all that extra weight also allows a spacecraft to go farther and faster. Some scientists believe that nuclear-powered rockets could travel to Saturn in just three years and make the round trip to Mars in a mere 200 days. Nuclear power has another advantage, too— endurance. Atomic energy could keep a spaceship going for years, long after conventional sources would have run out.

Nuclear rocket models have been built and tested. To date, though, no models have been used to launch spaceships. But the lure of quick space travel may change things quickly. Will that "small town with all the modern conveniences" someday also be a rocket ship cruising from planet to planet?

We'll just have to wait and see!

Is it Safe?

Despite many safety measures and procedures, nuclear reactors have presented some serious problems over the years. Power plants in Japan, the United States, and the former Soviet Union have all suffered accidents. The possibility of deadly radiation being released is always a concern. Some believe that nuclear-powered subs and rockets are a danger because of the atomic energy they contain. But so far, there has never been a radiation leak involving a nuclear sub. And some scientists argue that the risk of radiation from nuclear spacecraft is greatly exaggerated. In most designs, they point out, the rocket uses conventional means to escape Earth's atmosphere, switching to nuclear energy only later. And radiation is present in space, too, so the less time a rocket spends traveling through space, the more it reduces risk for its passengers.

Activity

ROOM TO MOVE Do some research into nuclear submarines. Find out the average number of crew members assigned to a submarine, and how much square footage is allowed for living space. How much living space does each sailor have? Then measure the living space in your own home, and divide it by the number of people in your family. Next determine the living space in your classroom. Sketching all three might help you get a better feel for the amount of space available. Compare the three: Which has the most space per person? Which has the least? What would it be like to spend four months in your classroom with your teacher and all your classmates?

Radiating from the Inside Out

In *X: The Man with X-Ray Eyes*, a science-fiction movie from the 1960s, a doctor treats his eyes with a dose of dangerous serum that lets him see inside his patients' bodies.

But that's science fiction. Here's science fact: Today, machines can actually look inside. And they use nuclear technology to do it. To help the equipment make images of the body's inner workings, the patients themselves are injected with radioactive materials.

Substances identified as "radioactive" send out invisible rays that can be dangerous to cells. Some can even cause cancer. But their properties can also work with sophisticated equipment to help doctors find out about medical problems safely, painlessly, and quickly. These procedures are used in a branch of medicine called diagnostic radiology.

If you break a bone, most likely your doctor will get an X-ray taken to find out what the fracture looks like. The X-ray beams that go in the patient's body are captured on film or by another detector to produce an image, explains Dr. Alison Haimes, a diagnostic radiologist in private practice in New York City.

Nuclear Medicine

Nuclear technology gets into the act with an even more hi-tech (and fast-growing) diagnostic procedure known as nuclear medicine studies. In this case, patients actually take in very small amounts of radioactive materials. While X-rays show images of sizes or shapes on the body's insides and can record changes over time, they can't show right then and there how different parts of the body are working. Nuclear medicine studies can take this extra step, says Dr. Haimes.

Nuclear medicine studies are extremely sensitive, so they can reveal problems that are too small to be detected by other methods. And an early, accurate diagnosis is important for addressing the problem effectively: The sooner doctors know exactly what's wrong, the better they can treat it. This greatly improves the patient's prospects for recovery.

Here's how nuclear medicine studies work: A patient swallows or is injected with a small amount of radioactive materials—also called radioisotopes or tracers. Which tracers are used depends on the part of the body being examined, because different materials are attracted to different organs, bones, and tissues.

The tracers travel through the patient's bloodstream to get to their destination. Once there, they send out rays that can be picked up by special cameras and recorded in a computer, which produces an image.

The radiologist's job is to analyze the images, along with the patient's medical history, to arrive at a diagnosis. "No one study can give you 100% of the information you need," says Dr. Haimes, "so I put together all the different pieces of the diagnostic equation. I love solving puzzles, which is really what it is."

Safety Zone

Although the idea of being injected with radioactive materials may sound scary, nuclear medicine procedures are actually safe because they use such small doses, she explains. Medical standards specify just how much radiation each body part is allowed to receive, and that level is tens of times higher than the amount of radiation used in diagnostic procedures.

Also, the radioactive tracers

don't stay in the body for long. The materials that are used have a short half-life, meaning that they decay to a harmless state within a few hours, and they are flushed out of the system through urination.

In fact, patients undergoing a diagnostic procedure are in less danger than the medical specialists who work with the materials day in and day out. For their safety, they follow strict rules and take daily precautions to decrease their exposure to radioactivity: They work behind walls of lead and leaded glass when performing nuclear medicine studies and use an instrument like a Geiger counter to measure radioactive leakage.

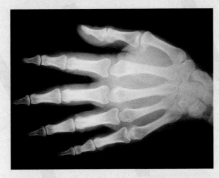

All radioactive materials are packed in protective lead shields. At Dr. Haimes's office, employees are checked each month to make sure that they are exposed to just one-tenth of the allowable guidelines for radiation. "We kind of go overboard, but it's worth it," says Jeanine Wyka, a nuclear medicine technologist who works there.

The benefits of nuclear medicine scans definitely outweigh the risks, she adds. "These tests can give the doctor so much information about the function of the body that cannot be picked up in other ways. You gain so much by using a small amount of radiation that's relatively harmless, doesn't cause any discomfort, and gives you quick results."

Explaining those benefits to patients is an important part of the job—and one of the most rewarding. "People are terrified when they come in for a test whose results will have a huge impact on the rest of their lives," says Dr. Haimes. "To be able to put a worried patient at ease, to get the best study we can, is a challenge—and a joy."

Ready for a Close-up

One of the latest nuclear medicine tools is the Positron Emission Tomography camera, better known as the PET scan. This can produce a three-dimensional computer-generated image of the entire body, rather than of specific sites. The radioactive materials used for PET scans interact with the chemicals in the body. As they decay, they release particles called positrons. These hit other particles, or electrons, in the body's chemical makeup. Both the positron and the electron are destroyed in the process. The reaction produces gamma rays, which are then picked up by the PET scan.

Because the PET scan can show system-wide activity, it is especially useful for finding out whether cancer has spread through a patient's body. Dr. Haimes's office recently installed PET scan equipment. Right away it made an enormous difference.

In one case, the PET scan clearly showed cancer that was too small to be confirmed by a CT scan. Without PET scanning, the patient would have undergone surgery so that doctors could take a sample of tissue, examine it, and make a diagnosis. With the PET scan, she avoided the risk of surgery and was sent immediately for chemotherapy.

In another case, the PET scan calmed the fears of a man who had cancer. "He was told he had six months to live, because cancer was found in two parts of his body," Ms. Wyka says. "We did a PET scan and saw that he was actually in good shape. The cancer hadn't spread, so he's a good candidate for surgery, which he definitely needs. But he'll make it through."

Activity

HOW MUCH IS TOO MUCH? **The U.S. government recommends that the maximum radiation doses for nuclear medicine technicians should be no more than 5 rems per year in their bodies (and 50 rems in their extremities, or hands). Imagine a hypothetical radiology clinic such as Dr. Haimes's office, and create a monthly chart to document radiation levels for each employee. (See chart on page 18 for more about rems.) Indicate on the chart the allowable levels for radiation, and plot hypothetical data collected each month for employees A, B, and C, measuring levels in their bodies and hands. Factor in that employee B is away from the office four weeks of the year, and also that employee A started at the clinic halfway through the year, while employee C is only working part time. To stay within 10 percent of the recommended guidelines, what should the maximum radiation levels be for each employee? By the end of the year, which employee has tested for the highest level? How do each employee's results compare with the recommended guidelines?**

A private company has been operating this mine for several years now, extracting uranium ore from the earth. The uranium is processed and made into fuel, which is used by nuclear power companies. But the miners have just stumbled upon a curious thing: a deposit of uranium that is not at all what it is supposed to be.

Preliminary tests reveal that this particular sample of uranium is practically worthless. Its useful properties have been stripped away almost entirely. The site manager is angry—in his view, this deposit of uranium is about as useful to him as nuclear waste.

You are a nuclear waste expert, called in to find out what this uranium is, and how it got here. You are working around the clock to answer the site manager's questions. Has there been some kind of foul play? Did a rival company, for example, plant some "useless" uranium in the mine in an effort to sabotage the operation?

You run some tests on the uranium sample. Sure enough, its makeup is off. Like other elements, uranium is a mixture of uranium atoms that have different weights. These "different" atoms are known as isotopes, and each gets its own number, based on its atomic weight. You expect to find two different isotopes in the sample: a very high percentage of one known as U-238 and a smaller percentage of another called U-235. Everywhere else in nature (even in rocks found on the Moon), the percentages of these isotopes in uranium is the same. Except in this sample. The percentage of U-235 is only half as much as it should be.

You can see why the site manager is concerned. Without enough U-235—about three percent— this uranium won't work in a nuclear reactor. Its atoms won't split spontaneously, striking other U-235 atoms in a chain reaction to generate the heat that is the basis for nuclear energy. The only other time you've come across such a depletion of U-235 was in samples of spent uranium fuel: in other words, samples of nuclear waste from power plants.

But how did it get here? After some asking around, you learn that there are no nuclear power plants anywhere near that area that might have secretly dumped the uranium samples here. Nor would any companies take unnecessary risks to transport their nuclear waste such a great distance. Also, the samples were found within the layer of uranium ore, under 200 feet (61 m) of porous rock—not exactly a practical location for nuclear waste!

A nuclear physicist has just published a paper arguing that nuclear fission reactions can take place in nature, without the mechanisms and procedures developed by humankind. You find it hard to believe, knowing how much engineering, physics, and careful attention to detail go into the construction and operation of a nuclear reactor. Something has to regulate the fission so it doesn't get out of control—our nuclear reactors use control rods and a coolant fluid such as water. What would nature do to sustain and control its own nuclear reactor? Is it possible that the sample is in fact "spent" fuel, only that it was spent in a natural nuclear reaction of some kind, not in a manmade nuclear power plant?

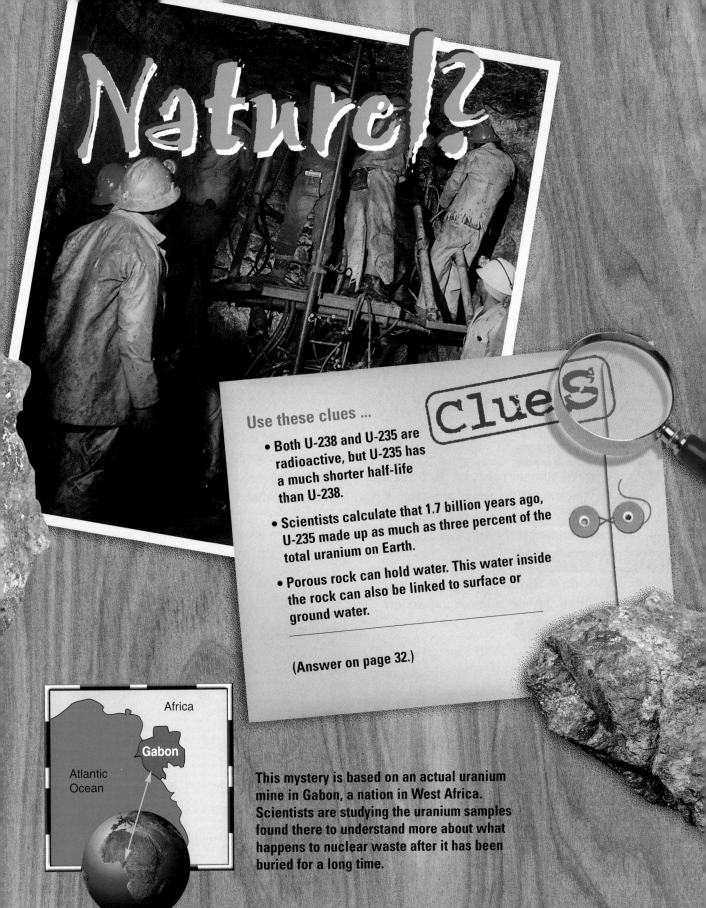

Naturel?

Clues

Use these clues ...

- Both U-238 and U-235 are radioactive, but U-235 has a much shorter half-life than U-238.

- Scientists calculate that 1.7 billion years ago, U-235 made up as much as three percent of the total uranium on Earth.

- Porous rock can hold water. This water inside the rock can also be linked to surface or ground water.

(Answer on page 32.)

Africa

Gabon

Atlantic Ocean

This mystery is based on an actual uranium mine in Gabon, a nation in West Africa. Scientists are studying the uranium samples found there to understand more about what happens to nuclear waste after it has been buried for a long time.

Gone Fission

NUKE TALK

A lot of phrases and expressions we use every day come from nuclear technology. This is why you won't come across terms like these in old movies or books.

CHAIN REACTION

When an atom of a radioactive element is split in the fission process, it gives off particles that in turn hit other atoms and split them.

CRITICAL MASS

You can't have a chain reaction without critical mass. This means bringing together a certain quantity of atoms of the radioactive element within a certain amount of space.

FALLOUT

Radioactive dust and debris that falls from the atmosphere after a nuclear explosion

MELTDOWN

When a reactor core gets too hot, it might result in a meltdown. This is when its fuel starts melting, causing damage to the protective casings of the reactor and escaping into the outside environment.

PLUTONIUM

Named after Pluto, the god of the underworld, this radioactive element is a by-product of nuclear reactions that process uranium. Plutonium can be used as fuel for making an atomic bomb.

NUCLEAR SUBPLOTS

Plutonium is a "natural" ingredient when it comes to putting together a plot for an action movie. Unfortunately, there is a lot of this dangerous substance around, and you don't need much to make an atomic bomb— 10 to 20 pounds (4.5–9 kg) will do. There are other creative ways to work with plutonium, as James Bond can tell you. In *The World Is Not Enough*, the British agent must stop a Russian terrorist from inserting just a tiny bit of plutonium into a nuclear-powered submarine's reactor. If the terrorist succeeds, the sub's reactor core will melt down, contaminating the entire Black Sea (and ruining the world's caviar industry in the process).

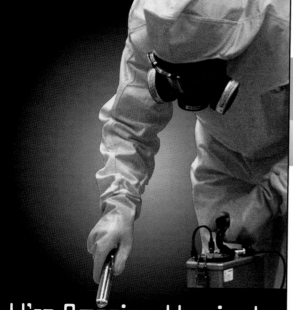

U're Amazing, Uranium!

Uranium, the element used as fuel in nuclear reactors, has a half-life of 4.5 billion (4.5×10^9) years. That's almost as much time as Earth has been around. Half of the uranium that existed on Earth in the very beginning of the planet is only now decaying into another element. That's why uranium is in such great supply. Much of today's uranium will be radioactive for another 4.5 billion years at least. But, think about it: Will Earth still exist at that time? Will we?

What Am I?

❶ I can't get through the first page of the Sunday paper. What am I?

❷ I can stay underwater for months at a time, and I don't need much to keep me going. What am I?

❸ Some might call me a "relative genius," even though scientific experiments weren't my strength. Who am I?

❹ I'm a chain reaction out of control. What am I?

❺ Without me, there IS no chain reaction. What am I?

(Answers on page 32.)

A Little Goes a Long Way

A nuclear submarine or aircraft carrier only needs a pound of highly-enriched uranium as its fuel. This is because an incredible amount of energy is released each time an atom of uranium is split in a nuclear reaction. And there are a lot of uranium atoms in a pound. How does uranium compare to gasoline? Let's count the ways: A ship would need at least 1 million gallons (3,784,000 l) of gasoline to get the same results as from 1 pound (.45 kg) of enriched uranium. Space is an issue, too: One pound (.45 kg) of uranium is smaller than a baseball, while 1,000,000 gallons (3,784,000 liters) of gasoline would need 125,000 cubic feet (3,538 cubic m) of storage space.

Nuclear technology has come a long way since it was first developed in the early 20th century. But one major problem remains: What do we do with nuclear waste? As you know from reading about it on pages 18–19, this matter remains radioactive—and therefore dangerous—for many years.

One day you and your classmates will be in charge of what happens on Earth. Perhaps by then new technologies will increase our options for addressing this problem. Imagine, for example, that we'll soon be able to load cargoes of dangerous materials onto rockets and send it out to space. Say the rockets could then return to Earth after ejecting their loads. It is your job to write up a proposal for shipping radioactive waste beyond our atmosphere and out of our orbit.

Gather your friends and teammates around and:

❶ Decide which waste should go first. More is being created every year, yet some reserves from the past are improperly buried in the ground or deposited in oceans. What would be involved if you chose to address the problem of old waste before tackling the issue of newly-created waste? Consider temporary storage facilities and where these should be located.

❷ Determine the best ways for transporting waste from dump sites or power plants to rocket launch centers. Consider the risks and benefits for each type of ground transportation.

❸ Evaluate the impact of such a plan on local communities. What are the dangers involved in transporting the waste from one site to another? Or of excavating waste that may already be posing a risk to residential areas nearby? Does the prospect of developing a permanent solution to the problem of nuclear waste outweigh these more immediate issues?

❹ Make a list of the supplies—including instruments and protective clothing—your employees would need.

❺ Assuming that the rockets are nuclear-powered and have roughly the same weight and power capacity as today's space shuttles, do some research and estimate how much enriched uranium would be required as fuel, per rocket. (See also pages 24–25, about nuclear submarines, and page 31).

❻ Sketch a basic plan for a rocket, indicating areas for the crew and the waste compartments. How would you design it to insure the crew's safety? What materials would be key to the rocket's construction? What are the dangers of placing radioactive materials in space? Consider the procedures and mechanics for ejecting the waste, once the rocket travels beyond Earth's atmosphere.

ANSWERS Solve-It-Yourself Mystery, page 28:

The answer is yes, this is a natural nuclear reactor. Or rather, it was. About 1.7 billion years ago, some sort of sustained fission reaction took place here. At that time, the U-235 content of the uranium was high enough and the surrounding conditions were just right to produce a nuclear reaction over a long period of time.

The "control" function was water, contained in the porous rock surrounding the uranium. This water source was most likely connected to surface or ground water. This constant supply of water acted as a coolant, keeping the fission from getting out of control, and also allowed the uranium atoms to continue splitting in a sustained chain reaction. The heat generated by nuclear fission heated the water and converted it to steam. Most likely, as the water supply within the rock was used up and replenished, the reactor stopped and started over a long period of time (perhaps over hundreds of years).

ANSWERS "What Am I?" page 31
1. An alpha ray, which can't go through a piece of paper
2. A nuclear submarine
3. Albert Einstein
4. An atomic explosion
5. Critical mass